ABOUT THE AUTHOR

Lexia Tomlinson is a poet, actress and spoken word artist who delivers captivating performances. Her work engages audiences with its unabashed honesty wrapped up in metaphors; she loves writing about life's personal and socio-political issues. Her central ethos is "the social is political, and the political is social, but everything is personal".

She has opened for the likes of Buddy Wakefield (A Choir of Honest Killers' tour), curtain-raised for a Kae Tempest play (Hopelessly Devoted) and was a 2017 Roundhouse Slam Semi-Finalist. She now concentrates on delivering excellent headliners at events and festivals such as Cheltenham Poetry Festival, Wychwood, Verve, Evidently, Headspace and Wilderness.

Her work has been commissioned by organisations such as MAC (Midland's Art Centre), WEP (Women's Equality Party), Beatfreeks and Birmingham Museum and Art Gallery. And has been published in multi-media digital formats such as Round House's 'Homing Pigeon', multiple zines and anthologies.

At the heart of it, Lexia cares about stories and people, anything that explores the human condition imaginatively; music, poetry, film, and activism are her main interests.

Sankofa is Lexia's debut complete collection of poetry.

Social Media Handles: @Lexialegend on Twitter and Instagram
Facebook Artist Page: https://www.facebook.com/LexiaTomlinson

Sankofa is a word and symbol from the Akan tribe in Ghana. In common translations the word means "go back to the past and bring forward that which is useful."

The word is derived from these words:

SAN (return),

KO (go),

FA (look, seek and take)

The Sankofa symbolizes the Akan people's quest for knowledge with the implication that the quest is based on critical examination, intelligent and patient investigation of oneself, and the world around them.

Lexia Tomlinson
Sankofa

VERVE
POETRY PRESS
BIRMINGHAM

PUBLISHED BY VERVE POETRY PRESS
https://vervepoetrypress.com
mail@vervepoetrypress.com

All rights reserved
© 2023 Lexia Tomlinson

The right of Lexia Tomlinson to be identified as author of this work has been asserted in accordance with section 77 of the Copyright, Designs and Patents Act 1988.

No part of this work may be reproduced, stored or transmitted in any form or by any means, graphic, electronic, recorded or mechanical, without the prior written permission of the publisher.

FIRST PUBLISHED NOV 2023

Printed and bound in the UK
by ImprintDigital, Exeter

ISBN: 978-1-913917-46-3

Cover illustration by Nina Sohal

*To the Universe
Past, Present, Future
Thank you for allowing me to unravel in
Devine Timing*

CONTENTS

PAST

Embracing The Elements of Air	13
Boomerang Kids	14
When you asked me for my trust but did not earn it	16
Make Way for Paradise	17
An Unhealthy Obsession	19
Ready	20
Harbour Wave (Tsunami)	21
Attempt at Three	23
How did God manage to destroy the dinosaurs on your watch?	24
All the colours	25
My Prayer	26
Stardust Blood Bath	28
Gutting Nerves	30
Chump Change	31
Every 10 Seconds	32
Obsidian Rock	34
Grey Scale	35
HAPPY	38
A Snapshot of Happiness	39
Beret Manifesto	40
All You Have Left	43

The Grim Reaper	44
Living Death	45
Man in His Infancy Forever Playing Hide and Seek with Biochemistry	47
The Nature of my Candour	48
To Drown at Sea	50
Gatekeeper to my Larynx	51

PRESENT

Clear Print I / *Clear Print II*	55
Dating Dilemma	56
The walk of shame	57
Crow Calling	58
Knowing	59
How I learnt victory was empty	61
When the dust settled	62
Steady Now	63
Ghee Whizz	64
The Original Manuscript	65
Make a meal out of me when you find the body	67
Breaking Birds	68
Arizona	69
Nairobi at night	71
They Take	72
Soft fruit	73
Ticking Time Bomb	74

Bleeding for some Goddamn manners	75
East of Eden	78
Boy is Lemon	79
Orange	81
Borrowed Time	83

FUTURE

Luna's Ruminations	87
(In the Fire)	88
Beanbag Skellingtons	90
Small Talk	91
Back To the Fairground	93
Only a Madman	95
The Artists Were Eating Grapes	96
Synonymous With	97

Acknowledgements

Sankofa

PAST

Embracing The Elements of Air

        We need to go back,
So far back,
        That we see everything seeping from Chaos...

I am like her, you once said
The Gap,
        Between Heaven and Earth.

They hold no relevance now.
Yet you still compare me to her.

There is no warmth in it.

I am your Erebos.

        When I only ever wanted to be your Eros,

Bringing you love and life.

        Now I will never be Aither or Hemera.

I will embrace night.
I will embrace me.

For I am Nyx.

Boomerang Kids

We're the boomerang kids.
Always returning to this fucked-up spot.
Except when were not,
But it all feels the same:
Neon, electric, flashing lights
Chrome
Bare brick
Hole in the wall
Megaplex
Spilt-drink, sticky floor,
Hormones, no place for subtle undertones
Tinnitus drowning bass.
The homebody in me is thinking "What a waste".
I want to be home reading, not have feet blistering or bleeding,
But in no time I'm retching, praying over porcelain
While bile is burning the back of my throat.
My world refuses to stop spinning,
I feel like I'm dying!
Bent double,
Promising God I won't do this again.

But Lying to ourselves is what we do best.

Because we're the boomerang kids.
We're yearning for something we don't have a name for.
So we blow what little we have on portals to the spirit realm:
Drink ourselves dizzy
Get mortal
Dance with Death and his Brother,
Hypnos and Thanatos.

Man do they know!
They know how to throw it down,
Make people wonder if you should slow down
No, make people judge that you need to slow down.
You know whilst their looking down at you from their great high:
Malibu, Mandy, Molly, Mushrooms,
Mary what you saying?

SHOTS, SHOTS, SHOTS!

And man do we knock em' back,
The booze and the boys.
But no free drinks for me,
Mamma and society say if I get roofied it's all on me.
Because obviously a woman's consent holds no gravity
In this society,
If anything happened it's my sobriety that would get questioned.
Not his sense of entitlement to a body that doesn't belong to him.
And as if to validate me
Unwelcomed hands snake out of the shadows to fly-swot out asses.
And automatically recoil to avoid accountability.
Tonight we don't fight with our fists or banshee scream over the music.
Instead we stop. Stare. And penetrate them with our eyes.
Only then do we keep it moving.
Up the river, like the motion of the booze in our bloodstream,
Ready to let loose I just want to dive into a beat
Let the rhythm flow through my uncoordinated feet.
Let the strobe lights baptise me in a sticky cacophony
Of smoke and sweat.

I could dance until I'm dead.
Thanatos whispers in my ear,
"That could easily be arranged"
But it's Hypnos that wins my favour
Pulling me onto his cushioned lap;
I'll close my eyes for a minute.
And that's all it takes for them to kick us out.

When you asked me for my trust but did not earn it

I stared at you
My mind conjured the image
Charon
Ferryman of the Underworld
Gaze so black, they looked like hollowed out sockets.
I can tell many secrets have set sail knowing only too well they will sink in you.
My death rites weren't paid so I don't feel safe to sing like a canary in silver to you,
Loose lips sink ships
I won't pay my 1/6th of a drachma
Just
To
Drown.

Make Way for Paradise

28 days into the New Year and your curved façade came crumbling down,
No longer would you be the beating heart of this town.

Spitting-up dust clouds in pleading protest
As cranes with their grapple teeth tear chunks out of you in a bid to lay your foundations to final rest.

Prometheus like in suffering, cursed, to witness the pecking of your own destruction.
Lobby's to save you were met with firm obstruction.

Yet the council wants to say it was you that was brutal.
"Too Insignificant" was their refute,
But they should have been clear about a place we held dear.
Say it was the plans for Paradise
That made them roll the dice,
The plans to be The Metropolis,
A chance to scrape off the concrete, step into the sleek
Be all glass; forget our crass past, reflecting down on London,
You can't smash these ceilings!

I want you to know you were anything but insignificant,
In your concrete cocoon I found my calling,
Youth Parliament meetings were I really thought I was going to change the world.
It was in your book-lined-belly I found my healing:
Escape portals etched into hardback spines
Sipping on re-hydrated hot chocolate in winter weather,
Breath so cold it created spectres of marshmallows in study rooms.
It was in those four walls I found a Poet's Place,
Learnt my craft,

Spit spells, read lines that created alchemy in my cells,
Glowing gold, fizzing for an elixir,
Knowing your gone makes me feel bitter.

An Unhealthy Obsession

An
unhealthy obsession
is a whirlwind
Tightly coiled around the spine
Of an artist
Scribbling pad.
Bold, black, biro
Runs rings around the silver steel.
Saturn would be jealous.
What is it you feel?
The easiest of the W's
Morphed into a why.
If I were you, it wouldn't be about expressing
I'd be all about squashing. Downsizing and repressing
like a girl of the world moving into a monastery.
Your art, so cheaply made,
Yet so expensively bought,
Makes me wish
That my unhealthy obsession of wishing
Would actually work for once.
I could click my sparkling ruby red heels
And be whipped-up in a
Mr. Whippy whirlwind.
And be deposited as a soft scoop in OZ
Where better than the Emerald City?
When the world has made me jaded.

Ready

Are you ready to forgive
Like you've never been betrayed?

Are you ready to love?
Like your heart has never been broken?

Are you ready to speak
Like you've never been silenced?

Are you ready to write
Like you've never drawn a blank?

Are you ready to listen
Like you've never heard before?

Harbour Wave (Tsunami)

There are days when a Tsunami of things unsaid swells in my sea chest.
I am afraid I do not know how to harbour there velocity
One day they will breach the Sea wall of my teeth
Foam on my tongue,
And flood the world around me.

My sister slips through the storm of my brewing solitude
"No man is an island".
She has watched me drown myself too many times to count.
I remind her I am woman,
I remind her I am always threading water,
I remind her Atlantis was full when it sunk.

There's a sea of sad in me that you can't see,
Endless Siren song,
Imprisoned somewhere here,
There, and everywhere.

I can't keep slicing my mind into pomegranate pieces.
Watching my aril gems pinched and pressed,
Sometimes there are no, sweet, hard pressed, victories.

I have a mind that is made up of melanin matters,
It is tired of being beaten and battered,
It screams, when you whip and whirl me like that I only end-up half-baked.

So today I will dress like it is summer;
Dress like I do not have a Hangman's noose around my heart.

Dress like I'm not a lobster; in my boiled black body shell, ready to be ripped apart.

Today I will dress like it is summer
So the Tsunami will stay away longer,
Leave so little material to cover me the cool air can kiss my tamarind skin.
So you can say I was asking for it and no one will question you.
Because I am asking for it,
I am asking you to look at me.

Woman, with the gravity defying hair, with skin the colour of fruit that cannot
Will not, make up its mind if it is bitter or sweet because it has found that's the only way not to be juiced of everything it has left.
You don't get to taste me,
You don't get to pollute the narrative of my personhood with angry propaganda
You don't get to disregard me or my people!

Attempt at Three

The Noughties, Blaire's Britain, Bali-bombings, world trade comes to a standstill.
As the terror attacks sink in.
All the people I know still dress like it's the Nineties.

I bounce around from designated kid's parties/ to sitting still at nameless aunties.
And I'm an alien trying to fit in, synch or swim.
But they're the weird ones, eating ice cream with Jelly.

"I shake it like Jell-O, and make the boys say hello". Blares from my sister's boom-box,
And haunts me into the playground, where all the girls try to 1, 2, step,
When the boys aren't around.

My face crumples into a frown.
"Come-on! How could you never have heard of The Magic School Bus?
I let it go. Never been the kind of kid to put up a fuss.

That must be why Isaiah thinks she can pick on me.
Mi wah lik di gyal suh hard she wih know fi nuh ramp wid mi.
But I take the high road, for now.

That means letting her pull my ribbons free,
Concrete grazed knees,
"No Mama, I'm just clumsy, of course, mi wouldn't let no gyal bully me".

How did God manage to destroy the dinosaurs on your watch?

The day the dinosaurs died could have been like any other Mother:
June afternoon, 16.2 degrees Celsius, hot and humid,
The kind of day that made you wish you could plunge into pools
Starfish spread on the surface of the water and float your way to heaven.

Except on this day the heavens had split at the seams, spilling destruction relentlessly.
Barrage after barrage of rainwater eclipsing the summer sun and smothering your Marigold's.
With nothing to do and nowhere to go God grew restless.

First he lined up his toy soldiers, drew lines in the cobalt blue of his suede carpet,
As they were about to fire he thought better of war.
But the dinosaurs were ripe for extinction,
He had grown bored of these backward plastic models,
The comet of commercialisation had convinced Godfrey
He needed the new ROBO-ULTRABOT 3000Tyrannosaurus Rex, Trachodon and Stegosaurus!

I couldn't stop him fiver year old fingers dashed mini dinosaurs that were once mighty in his affections into the fireplace he waited till night,
Its only when burning plastic crawled down my throat and threatened to choke me that I knew things weren't all right.

All the colours

God,
Splinters
Into 7 billion fragments.

"God help me". She prays

"There's no one listening you know." He says.

"You're just talking to yourself".

There is no Grey,
Just Black,
Just White,
And all the dancing colours.

My Prayer

It starts with the Lord's Prayer:
Our father, who art in Heaven
Hallowed be thy name.

Then it descends into the inane gibberish of my mind.
Asking questions, looking for signs.

I will never be as honest with another human,
As I am with God. I am told He know everything
About me anyway.

In my shoebox room,
A neon galaxy filters darkness,
A left-over legacy from a previous occupier.

In the darkness I search for the light
Seeking a guide for what is wrong or right.

I bear my soul,
Cry in confusion,
Discuss theories of evolution.
Tell him I've been taught to doubt
His very existence.

I have never doubted the existence of God,
The Creator, The Universe,
But I have doubts about religion,
Doubts about humanity,
Doubts about myself.

Am I good enough/Seriously good enough?
Am I worthy of heaven (if there is a heaven)?

I don't want to turn into one of those people,
You know the ones that only do good deeds to
Tip the scales in their favour.
Will your heart be heavier than a feather?
Or fed to an alligator...

Praying came so easily as a child, so too did honest good deeds.
Now tasked with providing my own daily bread.
Faith is held in fractions. Oh, how I wish to be whole again.

Stardust Blood Bath

Follow the bloodlines, percolating metallic silver soaking into the earth, emerald green glinting and rubbing rubies.
They bleed into each other.
I am the Lords living quilt. Call me melting pot,
The patchwork of pigments that is my skin is their story.
The story of colonisation and displacement,
Two things when you really think about it aren't so far from each other. The oppressor quashes his own soul in a bid to render your spirit to his bidding.

The weeping of my family tree tells the story of a Spanish woman
Who feared the melanin in her children's skin, is it because it spoke of her sin?
Her lustful un-doing. She raised her children perched up high on a white stone washed veranda, wide hat brimming out to block out the Jamaican sun. Trying to remain pale as possible. As for the children, they were not allowed to play in the day. The sun had to be set in the sky before they could run and scream.
I think a sense of her denial still lingers in me.

Then there is the Scottish-Man that ran away with a slave girl. As a child I was told I should be thankful for the red rust of my hair, his genes beseeched this to me.
I am more grateful for the dark brown the sun has oxidised it.

Finally, we have the slave girl, never born to be such a thing.
For thing is what you become when white men deem they can steal and buy you. Your original homeland I do not know.

I romanticised her and the Scots-man, the ultimate slaves to love.

These complex, cosmic creatures really do make me believe that each of us are the breath of specs of exploded stars.
There are many more stories in this quilt, one day I will track them down and wring them out.

But when the Rasta man confuses me for Kenyan I am not offended.
Is that where you were from slave girl?
When the black kids say I am not black enough
I will try not to get offended at their ignorance
When the white kids ask me why I am not black enough
I will try not to get offended at their ignorance.

If more people hunted down their heritage,
Instead of resting easy in the colour of their skin
To tell them where they are from.
The world would be a better place because they would realise
We are all melting pots, we have both been the oppressor and oppressed.
And one day you will just be another stitch in someone's quilt

Gutting Nerves

My
Smile Twitches,
Like a fish being flayed;
Scales licked clean off its body
By men wielding, serrated steel,
Terrier knives.
I
Am
Out
Of
My
Depth.

Chump Change

They say, whoever they are, that time heals all wounds; tell that to the keloid scars clumped together like jagged train tracks across my forearms. The silver scars smile in that broken way, the way a homeless man takes his cup of coins back to his chest and says "God bless" whilst on the inside, he's just waiting for one wintery night to give him eternal rest.

Every 10 Seconds

I see it clearly,
Calloused palm outstretched
Desperately clutching at dirty coins.
I bet he works hard to feed bellies he deems hollower than his.

I feel hazy
Two golden coins clamming up my hand
As I fondle them, flinging them around in my pocket
Like a methodical washing machine cycle.
I divert my eyes and walk on.
"God bless you" Follows me as the homeless man sits in his spot.

Sepia tones seeping at the seams,
The 9'O'Clock newsreel
Neutral face, biased voice,
Posters in bathrooms of service stations,
Gluttony and greed is good. Right?
Why else would they milk the tired and thirsty travellers for all they got?
Perfect marketing, empathy
Is it to make you think?
When you stop and stare at that poster directly above the sink:
Washing your hands with clean water, that runs into the mouth
Of the over-indulged-drain.
Red background, a child in black and white
A Western looking, white child, with the slogan
"A CHILD DIES EVERY 10 SECONDS"
Written in Times New Roman, Bold, Black, Size 72.
I know it happens here, you know it happens here.
But it doesn't, not really,
Does it?

I can't we have a welfare state.
They promised we'd be looked after from the cradle to the grave.

Giving is good,
Giving hurts when you cannot afford to,
Giving hurts when you want to
But don't.

Obsidian Rock

They say black don't crack,
So they say let me test that.

Black don't crack,
So they pushed hands down our throats and yanked out our foundations,
Trampled our flowers and ripped out our roots.

You won't crack, so we'll make you crumble.

What they don't know is we do crack, we do crumble,
But we come back stronger each and every time.

This is a resilience forged under 400 years of struggle,
Volcanic oppression on a magnitude you couldn't imagine.
It'll take more than that to make us blow out top.

Grey Scale

I sliced the amniotic fluid of the pregnant silence.
It leaked drip-dropped and wet the floor.
Enough was enough.
I would have to mop this up,
And wring the truth out no matter how much it hurts.

Sitting across the kitchen table from my grandma,
Hazel eyes burned into me like laser lights,
She cocked her neck and her lips fell apart in agape.

"My twin sister and I are a product of rape".

She let the words hang in the air,
They didn't need to be said with a dramatic flair.

"Or so we thought, I learnt the truth from my Mama before her passing.
Back in her day blanc and noir didn't mix to create a grey scale. It was a crime for a black man to love a white woman, so she told her papa what he wanted to hear so she wasn't shunned and turned away from the family flock."

"I'd rather be a black sheep any day than to be responsible for the persecution and death of the man I love," I muttered under my breath.

She shook her head in between that space of agreeing and disagreeing.

"That's so easy to say but we never lived in my mama's day."

The defense rose from the fire in her belly and smoked on her cheeks.
I sat back in my seat as if to say, I won't say another word,
give me the story.

"I came out the colour of barely burnt caramel and her clotted-cream,
So ended fairness and unities dream in this household".

The way my grandmother squared her shoulders and lifted her neck
I could tell trouble had made her bold and proud.

"She got the white hair and nose, only her lips were a little large:
I got hazel eyes and she got brown.
No one believed we were sisters around this town.

"One love, one heart." That's how we were supposed to be.
We would dance around with interlocking spurs for fingers listening
to Bob Marley. Creating crop circles on our cream coloured carpet,
But on graveled playgrounds that had a taste for the kneecaps of flesh
far too young. I felt the chains loosen and I knew her less and less."

Wishing I could catch hurt on the tips of my fingers
And turn them into raindrops to nourish drought-filled-lands,
I did the next best thing and offered a kitchen towel, smelling of citrus
fruit.

"She disowned me, and in turn, I learned to let her go.
That photograph you've got there in black and white,
Is the last we were seen together in the broad of daylight,
Holding each other tight, because she choose to be white,
And to her, that meant she couldn't have a Negro for a sister"

I'd never seen heartbreak reach out and choke a throat before.
I got up and turned on the radio.

"One love, one heart, let's get together and feel alright."

I cradled her to me and enveloped her in my arms like she was my grandchild. We danced until sunlight knocked on the kitchen window.

"One love, one heart, let's get together and feel alright."
"One love, one heart, let's get together and feel alright."
"One love, one heart, let's get together and feel alright."

HAPPY

Happy is evasive, we don't see her in this part of town anymore.
Happy is a fairy, (I'm not sure she exists).
Happy depends on your moods you starve her with your sorrow and rage.
Happy is tired of pretending, can't you tell? Nothing is okay.
Happy knows everybody wants her, but she isn't cocky,
Happy is letting you know if you want her you have to work for her.

A Snapshot of Happiness

Happiness, I have been told is far more elusive to capture and imbed between the lines of a page, than lovers, who really love, between sheets. Rarely do we stop to reflect back on the good times. We expect snapshots taken on the beach or at parties to do that for us. A picture will never tell the story of a three-hour journey: the muscle cramps, traffic jams; the umpteenth stops at service stations that delay our destination.

What the camera also fails to capture are the magical moments before the Click!

Such as our smiles or sense of triumph when we tasted sea-salt on our lips, heard seagulls squawk, slipped off our sneakers and the city to feel warm and wet sand on the soles of our feet. The looks we shared to say were finally here.

No, the photographs definitely don't capture that.

Beret Manifesto

Another weekend, another protest.
The crowd is dotted with the odd black berets or tired tie-dye T-shirts,
All who are wearing the fore mentioned have them tipped to the side,
If only they realised it wasn't just their caps that were skewed,
Bent, out of style and somewhat redundant.
"There is a war coming". The ringleader bellows.
His face fresh with youth not yet feasted on by fear
Or lined where death would have flirted,
Signals he knows not what he speaks off.
Fist-pumping, plunging in and out of the air, with vigorous rapture,
The innocent sky takes another beating.

Oh, all she has had to witness, is yet to witness.
The tales she will tell when her time comes to speak.
No wonder she is blue and black;
Burning up pink and bursting purple in the indigo eve, when she can bear no more.
No wonder the weather reports are always wrong.
They say nature is a woman, the highest of them all.
Our Mother, yet we dare to disrespect and destroy her.
No wonder why, no one likes getting caught in a winter shower,
When raindrops, launch like assault course spears and pierce our flesh,
For who can bear to see their mother cry, even if they do not like her?

"No, there isn't."
From the direction of stares,
It must have been a rolling internal heckle,
For all eyes were still locked onto
The self-proclaimed leader.
In his standard issue, lace up black boots, scuffed and marked unlike a soldier,

Un-washed army issue jacked purchased from Oxfam,
"There is no war coming, its always here, will always be here"
I want to scream until my throat is raw from the friction of the force
with which I bellow.

War is the mist that rises from blocks of dry ice
And in this grand play we call life,
The blocks have been placed into the wings of the stage
And every time they melt and the mist clears,
A time of clarity and harmony
Oh sweet peace.
Some stagehands with grand visions, their vision, not the ensemble's,
Cocks up the play by replenishing the ice.
In a different show, across town, I hear they have the same problem.

What do we do with problems? We try to solve them.
Leader 2.5 pushes leader 2.0 off his soapbox and promises
To make the air cleaner, across town;
The crowd cheers, not realising, or not caring
Ours isn't much better.
Can they not see this man is not qualified to be our director?
It's as if they've forgotten.
Even though the show must go on,
There is a war at home.

You take your eye off the ball
Next thing you know.
Own goal.
The director is now a dictator.

We trade in reality for a role every day.
Our senses for an act,
We don masks now,
When I shoot you in the heart, my mind doesn't want to witness
Lifelines ripping from your face.
So we agree to give up our rights to express how we feel
Thinking we're killing the enemy from behind our prisons.

Jim Morrison said it best.
"There can't be any large-scale revolution until there's a personal revolution, on an individual level. It's got to happen inside first."

I don't know how to end the war.
All I know is one universal truth is a lie.

All You Have Left

1. The ghost of your mother's kisses lingering on your forehead.

2. A rucksack with all your worldly possessions in it.

3. Your birth certificate and passport.

4. Those sandals you just had to get in the sale: the same sandals salvaged from the rubble of your room.

5. Your arms now your only comfort blanket.

6. Your beating heart. A soundtrack not even barrel bombs and dud drone beats could drown out

7. Memories: Adnan being a boy, his midnight black eyes sparkling like the stars just had to live there when he laughed, the smell of the lemon tree that stood for decades in your back garden and still stands defiantly, your grandmother's wrinkled hands trying to photograph your face to memory whilst she trips over Duas under her breath from going too fast.

8. 17 years of love. Playback moments on demand in the cinema of your mind.

9. Your feet. One foot after another (just keep moving)

10. Hope. You will find her at the bottom of your backpack; she always hides in the darkest of places in the darkest of times.

The Grim Reaper

When the veil ripped/(Open)
All the souls slipped/(Out)
They floundered and filtered.

He carried me (Carefully)
Like I was water.

Loosing
        parts of me
                along
                        the way.

Living Death

Death is young, ageless and infantile,
Yet the joints in his knees crack
And creak.
To concede would be to tell a lie,
that he is weak.

Death and Life have a wager.
Who has it harder?

The day Death was born:
Mother Nature grew grey with worry,
Bags of black clouds formed in her eyes;
And birthing waters lashed down-upon
The earth. Her cries were echoed in thunder,
The ground shook,

Rules were being broken.

Death is a beautiful baby.
Alabaster white;
He will take on characteristics of stone,
Easily mouldable yet strong inside.
His eyes are the darkest brown,
His eyes will become cups of coffee
Girls will want to sip instead of swallow and run.
His hair is a soft sea of black curls
Languidly lying on each other.

His body is soft, warm,
Everything you want to hold dear
Lavish with hugs and kisses,
Death is loved.
Death is six:

He is puncturing the palm of his mother's hand
With fear, in the form of crescent cuts.
"But I don't want to go to school"
He does not need to go to school.
Not only has Death moonlighted as wisdom,
He has conversed with every passing soul.
Why else did you think people were living longer?

Man in His Infancy Forever Playing Hide and Seek with Biochemistry

I'm a Rubik's Cube of biochemistry
Twisting and turning, continually
Never quite solved.

"Surely there is nothing more beautiful than this?"
One scientist ponders aloud.
Greedy, glinting, grass green eyes
Shimmered like heat waves dancing.
It reminded me of the undulating snakes
That had been charmed by man.
And to the time when men had no
Right to a name; just nomad. Wandering the desert.

I pulled the future out of the North wind.
"Specimen to be studied? No. I am not."
The light bulbs in his eyes explode like the lights
on old Broadway, smashed to signal the death of a star.

We are free because this world is still unfinished but
This thirst for knowledge might drown us al

The Nature of my Candour

I sit stoic as stone,
I watch life because it has not watched me
Instead it left me, deserted, alone.

My eyes catch an insignificant Bee,
I release it from my gaze,
There is something quite free
In spending your life in a transparent haze.

However, I prefer the pessimistic view,
When you fall under the radar
Not even the highest sonic frequency
Can find you.
No one wants to find me.
I'm not even a glimmer of a second thought,
What wrath, what curse did I bring upon myself?

The answer is simple.

I was born a cripple
Do not pity me any physical deformities,
For I have none.

I am crippled by Nature, by Society
Lacking in social grace,
And bound to my place!
The day I was born they tied me in black lace.

Since then the lace has evolved,
And spread like a viral disease, over
My skin, wrapped around my
Tongue and rotted it away.

The soul is also in a state of decay,
All I have to do is cut the lace,
But it connects me to the Human race,
I look down though; and there's already a fray.

I am se-v-er-ed.
Strung-up and pulled apart
Unravelling at rapid speed,
I am so close to being freed

I can smell it, not taste
For you make mistakes when in haste.
The lace shreds, I don't disappear
In fact for the first time I appear.

"Speak, Speak, Speak"
"Squeak, for Freak Sake, spit-it-out!"
I have no tongue, yes, but I have
 Voice in pen, one that is highly strung.

I am marvelled at my candour
But no longer shall I remain in
The shadows;
Feeling down and dour.

To Drown at Sea

My Mother is planning another escape.
I can tell,
Her eyes take on that doughnut-glazed expression,
And they dodge mine like a ninja,
Slipping through a bamboo forest.

She swats the empty air
Scratches at her skin until its red raw.
No easy feat
On skin the colour of
Waxed mahogany.

I keep telling her
There is no sea inside this apartment
But that won't stop her from drowning.

Gatekeeper to my Larynx

Why are you afraid? I just want to hold you,
So the sharp kiss of my steel
Can split the seams of your spine.

Fear said she wouldn't play xylophones with my ribcage tonight,
She said she wouldn't dance like a Cobra
Weighing up its prey before the strike
She said she wouldn't bite until the moment was right,
Until I was ripe.

Fangs noshing, fork tongue flickering
She is drowning on the moistness of her saliva
And I give in to her
Always so weak-willed when it comes to her.

I just want to be naked.

As I scrutinise my reflection
I realise it's so easy to stand bare
We can all peel off pieces of clothing
It's no longer a sacred thing.
But I'm dying, to step-out of my skin
And be the being I was in the beginning.

I want to see the source
I want to touch the source

I imagine it will look like a Nova Star
Cataclysm of sparks flying,
Burnt oranges
                        Electric Blues
And red Hues

So I inhale brave and exhale fear. I've been lying to you.
But more importantly I've been lying to me.
I've been conditioned by society to be what they want me to be
So much so
That I don't know how to
Just
Be.

Fear has been the Gatekeeper to my larynx for far too long.
I've concocted a formula for fitting in.
Smiles that strain the structure of my face.
This is a standing sea wave pattern engraved on the seabed of my skin.
And I'm so seasick of going through the motions
Nodding to things I don't even agree to!

I bite my tongue most days until it bleeds:
So I'm not offended when I overhear
Strangers saying my breath stinks of iron.

I rust when exposed to too much oxygen.

I am not used to space to breathe in.

I am afraid my opinions have grown pleasing, placid and agoraphobic,
I am afraid to tend to my flock, so I put on my wool and lay in the field
With my sheep.

Sprinkle me with kerosene, burn this body on a heap.
Let me be reborn with no inbuilt censoring alarm.

And the voice asks me again. What are you afraid of?"
And I finally know,
It's to the potential to be powerful beyond all measure.

PRESENT

Clear Print I

Have you ever watched a man walk through water?

Watched him until his footprints disappeared ...

Until he became one with the concrete.

Clear Print II

I watched a man walk through water,
Until his footprints became one with the concrete.
I saw him look up, to meet the skyscrapers.
They were scattered like wild flowers and broken teeth.
He just stood there staring,
Letting the rain piss on him.

Dating Dilemma

If I'm the one ghosting you, why are you the one haunting me?

The walk of shame

A rubbish bag vomits on the concrete:
The scent of cracked eggshells echoes up,
And the seagulls descend.

The Earth is a bruised body,
Blue, oh so blue. Erupting the caverns,
Coughing up black smoke.

We are living out her dying days.
Resources mined to the brink.

Go on, laugh at her lack.
Ask, "How dare you crack."
She's supposed to be the strongest of us all
Down there at the bottom of the pyramid.
Black bird. Woman, black bird. wings clipped.

Crow Calling

All we humans seem to sing of is love.
Yet our actions are the antithesis of those siren songs.
Since recorded history there have only been 250 years of peace.
The Earth is 4.5 billion years old
Let that sink in ...
Like a tectonic plate submerging beneath an oceanic one,
I'm no doctor, I do too little.
But if interspecies translations were possible,
It's only fair to assume that bird songs are about war and flight.
The dawn choir that disrupts your sleep is a war call.
A council of crows cluttered together,
Discussing how to best take back the Earth from fallen guardians.
They chirp and chatter about the air,
They speak of how their wings, wrinkled, streaked and spotted by pollution
Refuse to become like Skellig's, when we are gone these wings will sprawl out
And glide on the wind. On a wind that is neither supporting nor hindering.

Knowing

The world is turned down to number five on the TV.
It feels like 5am
In spring before the sun fully comes up.

The sky is languidly lingering between a bleached-blue-sweater
With splotches of tangerine/
When she spills pink pop
And lavender crumbs on herself.
The crumbs flake through the cracks of the skyline.

I can taste their residual warmth on the tips of my fingers.

A squadron of blackbirds late for the dawn choir quarrel
   On till
       Their all
            On the same key.
I let the silence breached only by birdsong, bathe over me.

It is not 5am.
It is not spring.

You have missed that season
Two weeks late, I'm not sure if this is a precursor of things to come:
A pattern etched in your DNA,
I don't know you, yet.

A heady romantic,
I fall in love with strangers everyday:
I imagine that fast volley of eyeballs bouncing back and forth
Is a game kindred's play.

I do not have to imagine that I love you.

I've been told that heartbeats can be synchronised.
And I've always assumed that people saying, "I would die for you",
Was taking the easy way out; because we all know living is harder.
Why else do you think that the exit routes located on the tops of
skyscrapers and thin ledges look so damn attractive?
Especially when you have vertigo!

But now I know...

I would crack the cages of my ribs
Hear them snapping like spaghetti sticks,
Know how twigs feel under the force of feet,
For you to live.

Why are there not separate hospitals for the living and dying?

A bug like buzzing
(Buzzes)
And the hiccupping of the machines
Pull me under
The riptide of the endlessly white-washed corridors.

The summer sun streams through the windows,
Spotlighting you.
Womb wrinkled,
So old and yet so new.

How I learnt victory was empty

My cousin and I are six, and we have a score to settle with each other. The other children stand on the sidelines as we draw a line in the sand.
Red earth, dried by the orange sun, hitched a ride on my bare brown feet.
It leaped into the air. My white dress already tarred and marred took another coating. I stared at Janelle. Our eyes met and locked in competitive mirth.
We twinkled at each other. Looking back out down the dirt track, target assessed.
"Ready, Set, GO! We squealed in high pitch unison. We were running in our little black bodies oh so free. My body absorbed the shock of the earth and turned it into heat. At the bottom of the lane was her mother waiting with open arms.
I won but there was no one to embrace me.

When the dust settled

My mother came back for her child.
Only to find I was a shell-shocked Cinderella,
Hair turned to copper.
Rusted neglect haloed around my head.
Clothes tattered, bones protruding,
Childhood chubbiness
Used as survival stores.
And the once, often kissed cheeks gone.

Steady Now

The table seesaws on unstable legs,
Unhinged somewhere inside you can't see.
Your initial feeling is to fix what is broken.
The table wonders how
a broken person
can fix a broken thing.

Ghee Whizz

How deep is your love – Gushes out of the radio faucet,
Making a pool out of our situation.
I flip the dial,
But the Bee Gee's are waiting.
Robin Gibb goes in for another silky falsetto:
"How deep is your love?'
"How deep is your love?"
"How deep is your love?"

The room is rapidly filling up
We're treading water, egg-beating tired tongues
Inside of arid mouths.
No one says a word.
Even if the words could be a life raft.
So we drown in uncertainty and insecurity.

The Original Manuscript

I like to blow hurricanes and whirlwinds into my tea,
So that I can fool myself that I am swallowing sorrows.

I imagine that's what God does.

I also like to imagine that the 'Great Flood', was him spilling coffee
On the final draft of his manuscript;
Because he knew it wasn't good enough.

I mean, why in the grand scheme of things can't God have a pushy editor?
The whole 'fire and Brimstones' thing...
An over-zealous director who wanted to make Sodom & Gomorrah into a "Block-Busta"!
You heard that right folks, not 'er'.

We should all know by now, you can't start a story the way it should end.
Paradise, utopia...
That does not make for good reading. I mean where's the plot development?

I feel sorry for God,
Noticeably absent
But always to blame.

The Devil gets a lot of screen time. "He made me do it", is an instant one liner.
Like "He'll be back".
Am I talking about The Terminator or the Messiah?

I started to feel sorry for God after The Simpsons and The Sims:
Tree House of Horrors VII, Genesis Tub, Lisa became a God
without knowing it.
I thought we could all be some kid's school project.
An entire planet in a petri dish.

I felt sorry for God after playing The Sims day and night for
six-weeks-straight.
Here are these beings of pixelated perfection
And all I think about is how to destroy them.

I felt sorry for God after Inception, he's playing me, and The Sims
are playing Tamagotchi. Or are the Tamagotchi playing The Sims,
playing me, writing about God?

I felt sorry for God when I thought of him as a writer, no *the*
writer, The Creator and the Omega.
I mulled over him being an author, then I chose to rip pity from
the beating heart he gave me and replace it with empathy.

My pixelated pets and people do not have the gift of autonomy.
They love and hate at my whim.
Push and play.

Imagine the game never stops
Imagine they have free will...

Make a meal out of me when you find the body

Starvation smells like a rotting corpse left exposed to the summer sun.
Back then I was always chewing, chewing, chewing gum,
But my mother would always burst my bubble.
Artificial strawberries couldn't mask my bad breath,
Artificial citrus couldn't bless me with confidence.
Artificial peppermint couldn't make me cocktail-stick-thin,
But then again neither did binging and purging.

Breaking Birds

You asked me how they break Falcons.
Left arm log stiff,
Looking like refuge from the summer sun
Looking like stable
Looking like home to my wondering soul,
And you already know,
You know how they break birds like me.

Arizona

Sometimes, I think the people I love most dead.
And I love. She sips.
Me.

Arizona is disappearing, submerged under the tectonic plates of gin and tonic

Arizona is disappearing in the arid desserts of her jaw
Cottonmouth
Molly mouth
Gin drought

Arizona is disappearing and everybody is cheering.
Just keep going

The finish line is hooked into the hollow of her clavicle.

She's hooked on the gurning you can only get from music.
The floating silence
The slipstreams that steal her days

It started when the women...

The women called the boys down,
Down to the river,
Gone where the spit baths
Tongue to thumb
Thumb to tongue
Thumb to eyebrow
Thumb to cheek

The boys will grow up
Fascinated by spit.
How it looks
Lubing their skin
They will beg girls to be licked clean

The girls were left
In a room
You think you know the room.
But all cells are different.
They will listen. Ear pressed hard against solid wood.
They will always burn to be heard

Nairobi at night

Heat hums in the atmosphere,
Weighing down my body
Yet slackening my limbs.
I know how the stars feel tonight.
Restless to shine,
They try to poke holes through the smog
Of pollution,
Only to be catapulted back under
The thin sheen on the night screen.
Somewhere in the distance a tap gurgles
Constantly like a brook;
She is calling for the rain clouds to break ranks,
And dance with playful abandon on Zinc
Topped roofs.
I wait,
Heavy lidded,
For the rain.
For the three bouncing dots.
One never falls...

They Take

There are parts of me that want the sadness. Has no wish to relinquish the darkest.
Doesn't toy with the with the idea of pressing the red button but schedules self sabotage,

 5, 4, 3, 2, 1

Offer myself up to the demons because it doesn't matter how fast I run, in the past I never won. But if I stand still I'll know what's to come.

I'll let him kiss me
I'll let him fuck me
But I won't let him love me.

I don't think he knows how,
And I've always liked giving more.
So take, take.

Oh wait, you already mined my heart like the Portuguese plundered the gold coast in 1471
And now you're back this summer all charm, but your just more harm like the British in 1867. Is it going to take me 90 years to be independent of you?

Soft fruit

I am tender here,
Nort-West of my groin.
You bit me here,
And growled "mine".

I am tender here,
90° of my right eye.
Trust, punctured there,
Blame belongs to wine.

Ticking Time Bomb

We were a jumped-up constellation of loose change; I would have handed mine all in to pay for the vacuumed silence. The humdrum of a day going nowhere.
The humdrum of a heart laid bare.

In the aftermath, the sun came up and I was looking at you.

I couldn't tell you I'd already mourned you. In the vision I was white hair wise, more wrinkles than skin; but the breeze still flirted with my cheeks. Yet I could hardly feel it's' kiss because yours lingered from the grave.

You told me you planned to be dead by thirty.

Never thinking how that would hurt me.

So I pulled the plug on a lifetime of longing.

Erected a fortress between our bodies, rolled off the mattress and glued myself to the door.

Called-us-error, called-us-mistake. Flung faults in your face, behaved in a way that would cause distaste.

Peeled back the paint on our pairing and confronted you with your casket.

Do not ask me to love a dead man walking.

Bleeding for some Goddamn manners

POETRY HAS NO GODDAMN MANNERS!
No sense of timing, but she knows...
She burns with that white-hot-heat of urgency.
Unyielding and demanding, she will not relent
Until you stand-back, Shell-shocked,
Wondering why you're not in a PADLOCK
CELL-BLOCK!

Would you have her any other way?
Would you have me any other way?

Last night I looked-up and found the answer,
Dangling from The Web, the whisper of a strand
Spun from a spider.

The clues had been there for weeks,
Bleeding into months.
I could feel them, each time a new sore appeared
In the festering mountains of my skin.

Scratch till the skin bleeds
Scratch till the skin bleeds
Scratch till the skin bleeds

Run river run   (Sung)
Run river run

Scratch till the skin bleeds

And it feels like syrup, running down my leg;
Charting unwatered terrain
Warm and wet.

I know I should stop.

The other bruises don't speak up for you though.
They want you to be tainted just like them.

I know I should stop because you want me to keep going.
So you can be fucked-up.

But guess what?
You're already a Fuckboy
So there's really no saving you!
And I could swim before I was born
So let me cut this umbilical connection.
Don't get it twisted!
There's nothing maternal about my affections for you,
I just get tangled –up in metaphors like you get snarled in paintings
And insects in webs.

Before we know it we're shrinking,
Cocooned in something/someone we never wanted.
I choke on pieces of you daily,
You are acid-reflux.

Do you choke on me? Do I rot somewhere in your intestines?

If you answered yes to two, here are some lyrical laxatives
Because your actions already treated me like the proverbial do-do.
Yet all I do is reiterate to my friends that I don't hate you.

I don't have you.

Abrupt ending and cliffhangers just leave an unsavoury taste in my mouth.
Could-have-been plays on loop in the empty cinema of my mind.
You once told me I couldn't stop you from being my friend if I tried.

I never tried.

Oh, this Goddamn spider won't stop biting me!

East of Eden

I was always a ghost,
Accepted that my body was dust.
Before Earth,
Ever even tasted like a memory of Eden.

Boy is Lemon

Boy is lemon
Boy is always lemon.
Boy is bright, bold, black, and brunette

Boy will suck you in like fresh lemonade
On a long hot summer's day.

Boy black is always high
He speaks in 11, universe, stars
Shuttle ships and sharp hiss.
Boy black is all bark and no bite.
He's not the one, I stay-up,
Thinking of at night.

Boy bright is blonde
Only his hair is light,
Heavy is the head.
Inside he is cornfield blue.
The secrets in his sleep
Slip out in mumbled disarray
He will keep lying.
"I'm Okay".

Boy bold has no identity,
He is a beard.
Beard boy is a hollowed-out
Carving, bitter wood chips,
He's one flint spark from
Exploding! When he looks
In the mirror he says he sees his father
He doesn't know where he begins and ends.
Boy bold is borrowed time.

Boy brunette is lemon.
He bites hard, piercing and bursting
Rigid rings of rind to find the truth
The kind of truth that is bright like bleach
He scrubs through the stench of self-hate,
Realises every time he self-deprecates
Another chunk of his soul he annihilates.

Boy is lemon, but cannot be found here.
The one I seek is burning juice, you know the type
The ones that make you just want more
The one.
You know the one, he is bright, bold, firm
Yet, soft inside. The one that makes you
Stay for a second sip.
The one that makes you taste the sweet behind the bitter.

Orange

He peels off my woman like expert fingers do to satsumas in their orange suits.
Under hazel eyes I'm a translucent sac of girl again.

I'm a little worse for the wine and weed but they lubricate my inhibitions,
Let the hinges of my pelvis gyrate their timeless need.

Under his single duvet the bread of our bodies bake.
Hands splayed in surrender search reverently
For spaces in need of kneading.

And, Ping!

The text-tone brings me back to flesh and bone.
The lights are on and all the ideas are home.

I remember the talks with the God, others call Grandma.

"How do you know you've learned your lesson if you're not tested,
Time and time again?"

I leap from the bed like a cat who wears distrust for fur,
Glue myself to the only thing that is right,
Stabilise sea-sick legs in the corner of the door.

"Do you feel the history?" Watch with weary eyes.

"Do you feel the history of us?" Ask with wounded pride.

I follow the flashback in your eyes of me giving birth
To poems, on your floor ...

"Do you feel the history of this moment?
Vesuvius, we ain't erupting now! Do you hear me?"

Boy, you could have been Jesus.
What, with the way you walked
On the wounds on my heart like water.
Boy, you could have been Jesus.
What, with the way you dodged my questions
Turned it into your own.
"Wine?"

And I am left to peel the rind of my senses of the floor
Cloth myself in youth.
Dear God,
I have learned my lesson.

Borrowed Time

It is midnight
In me.

In Elysium, those that can remember say, "the Sun never sets".
Immortal generator, she hums at 20 Hertz,
If you blink you won't hear Her, but our skin,
Our glorious skin, that magically intuitive organ
Will perk-up its ears and tune into the Suns frequency.

(Skin is always desperate to be kissed by the sun.)

Skin will dance a kaleidoscope of ribbons to her tune,
Here on Earth we merely call them "Goosebumps".

It is midnight
Outside of me.

The crooked crescent hanging by a thread in the sky confirms this.

I am sat on the island of my single-bed, tracing crop circles into my skin
Fingers skimming over the ridges of goose bumps like a smooth stone bouncing on waves,
I am 22 and I don't know what the fuck to do.

I want more from Chronus than he is willing to give to any human,
I remind him of the boy Bernard. "What about his watch?" I plead.
He spits back at me, "FICTION".

Fact,
Is the God's don't speak to me anymore not the way they use to,
I'm filling in the missing dialogue like an actor doing a duologue

Maybe I should just make this into a one woman show endless monologue.

I'm not sure the God's ever spoke to me.
I'm not sure of many things
And it's with that admission that the damn of doubt bursts.

Every day I fray and fracture a little bit more,
Here on Earth we call them wrinkles,
Every day I drown in my own decisions
Here on Earth we call them consequences.

I stopped competing,
Wished my heart would stop beating,
Not knowing the only reason your garden was growing greener was because you were watering them with your tears.

I've never told anyone about the times I tired of earth
Searched endlessly for exit routes and portals on the tops of abandoned carparks,
Looking for the end.
Always reminded of beginning

FUTURE

Luna's Ruminations

In the beginning, there was Choas;
from her primordial waters, we seeped
I won't tell you where she came from.
What sound or speck created her,
for this is my story.
All I know of the universe;
That I will tell you,
Involves what I have seen,
heard and felt.
I have lived long enough to be worshipped.
I have lived long enough to know;
That I, too, will be disregarded and cast aside like other Titans,
when the mystery is no more.
I will live long enough for Mankind to run rope-rings
around me; like Humpback Whales in the Antarctic of
their planet hunted to extinction.
I will live long enough to feel the sharp spike
of pickaxes break my surface and create more craters;
feel my body being broken and shaped to their will.
Watch myself colonised without the strength to shake
them off, as we all watch Earth burn.

(In the Fire)

Fear mingled with foresight like an uncontrollable blizzard,
I stood in the swirling snowstorm of my vision picturing the
glorious un-hinging of my heart before I'd even run my first mile
Yet here I was, dressed before the dawn, in all black like I had something or someone to mourn.

Feet meet concrete, I mumbled, like they weren't long aquatinted acquaintances
Feet finally meet concrete: but really it could have been grass, gravel, or any given street; as long as I had a place my body could travel at full throttle
Here I could act like a baby, preconceived notions of dignity thrown out the pram
Scream at the top of my lungs "Who hell do these people think I am"
Pant like the lapdog I know they take me for, whilst I pick up the pace at the fork tongue
Remind myself it won't be long until I return leader of Pack.
So keep throwing me to wolves

So I mantra:

Go baby Girl

Go baby Girl

Go baby Girl!

Hone your growl, bare your teeth at every single stranger you meet in the park, don't flinch when the too, too big dog starts to bark. Yell "good morning" through the frost; wait for the songbirds to chirp their reply
Master meandering between the states; past, present and it's never too late.

Become okay with the fact that you won't always know the right way

Trust your thighs of thunder, soon they will rain down like Usain Bolts', let your tears fall freely but wipe them quick like sliver, continue on your journey Mercury, because you've always had a message inside of you but you're only just learning to tell it
 Let the unspoken pains and power flow through;

This is therapy

Spluttering and coughing until I'm both gasping and glowing
I stared-up at the trees that had begun growing their gowns green for summer, they shone with the highest saturation of sunlight yet somehow this was my photosynthesis.
I inhaled deep into my chest to quell the blazing fire only to laugh out a smoking cackle at how others thought this was about getting into a smaller dress, potential lovers to impress or any of that other superficial nonsense.

This is a metamorphosis,
And sometimes a caterpillar yearns to be more than a butterfly!

Beanbag Skellingtons

Dear Love,

Tonight we are twin polar peaks of the same shoulder. East coast to West coast of collarbone.
We are alone. Know when we get in the other won't be home.
Know you're not a number to phone.
Instead. Tonight, I will wander past the hoards, linger too long on couple cradled in the corner.
Skellingtons sagged like empty beanbag mountains on top of each other.
I watch their fingers cat-cradle into geometric shapes of companionship. Watch the signs of their language like I used to on Saturday mornings during the BBC2 deaf take over. I'm shut out from the sign language of their love but I still admire it.

Nothing ventured nothing gained.

I'll keep looking for you in bodies that are not your own. Catch glimpses of your spirit, finally think this is it. Only to have the carpet pulled out from under my feet. And have the magician wave his cape like a matador. Perfect illusion.

With one mistake I'll even get close to the mirage of marriage.

Yours faithfully,

Small Talk

We make small talk;
Crawl between the spaces of time/

And we're children again, hiding in the crawl space of your brother's cupboard
Where nobody can find us, pin-pointing galaxies and poking pins into paper maps,
Picking out all the places we'll explore.

We make small talk
/Slip off our sneakers and run- down memory lane until we run out of things to say to each other. (Gasp)
(sharp intake of breath)

"Remember when?" (Pause)
Is cue for a drawn- out game of ping-pong playdough
Where brows become so furrowed they resemble a karesansui Garden.
We're wracking our brains trying to rake back memories that bonded us together.

And no doubt, No Doubt's 'Don't Speak is the diegetic backing track softly bleeding into our consciousness, in our corner of the café all the goodtimes, easy conversation and spontaneous giggles seem so far away.
And I'm wondering if this is the Central Peak in our Perk
I feel like the used teabag clinging on for shelter on the side of your saucer,
If only this distance was something we could conquer.

I really feel
That I'm losing my best friend
I can't believe
This could be the end
Silence
Was always a home we sheltered in together,
"Don't Speak, I know what your thinking!"
And that's what scares me
So I sip my ice coffee that was hot when we sat down. And you shift your gaze anywhere but to mine
You're not Israel and I'm not Palestine
Yet, there's definitely a gaping wound,
Sometimes Empires fall;
Without a catalytic conflict
We're the crumbling ruins of the pain neglect inflicts.
I
Really
Feel
Like
I'm
Losing
My
Best-
Friend.

Back To the Fairground

The fossilised bone is brushed-back-over,
    I regurgitate the magnificence of the cliff-face:

Unfurl my body; walk away from the beach.

Spit-out the taste of sea-salt
Before I even get the chance to smell it.

I'm back on the coach.
Where my leather seat is memorising the knots and curves of my back
When it succeeds, I sigh and squirm in contentment.
I watch the views of the Isle blur:
It's a slideshow of green-blue-grey,
Nothing ever comes into focus.

I quell the excitement inside of me that had my left-leg bouncing
    Up and down like a tennis ball.

The fire in my lungs is exhaled as frost,
It is sill smoke;
Fired-up or flat, air will find a way to float in one form or another.

I cacoon myself into my quilt, rub my face against its familiar flannel face,
Comforted by its all-consuming embrace. I imagine this how my cat feels
when his face is nuzzled in the warmth of my palm.

I turn the lights in my mind down.
Tonight the flashing lights of the fairground won't bombard me.
I will not go-around-and-around in the Spinning Teacup.

The concept of guilt is erased,
Like a rubber taken to pencil and paper.

I never said the words at the tip of my tongue

Only a Madman

Only a Madman would have painted this

Is printed in pencil onto my canvas of the The Screaming Man.
Mad man.

The eternal scream.

I painted out my soul for you to see.
For you all to see.

At the unveiling room the critics and the well-to-do room whispered.

The walls wouldn't, couldn't, stop whispering: hands in brightly coloured gloves,
covering mouths sucking and sinking my psyche.

I wilted under their stares.

I had already painted out everything. So only the words were left to etch.

The Artists Were Eating Grapes

I looked over my shoulder and observed them,
In many moments montaged in my memory.
Some swallowed rejection like a toxic-tonic;
It filled them up with bitter resolutions.
Some chewed the meaty olive flesh of rejection.
The smart ones knew to grip the seed
Between their teeth and spit it out;
The smart ones know/They always know
To consume only the things which nourish you.

They are fire-breathers;
that pour water onto crackling embers
For fun.

Watch as smoke and steam
Evaporates into the indigo-eve,
And describe it as:
The release of a soul.

Synonymous With

I am Girl.
Straddling the cusp of womanhood,
On shaking Bambi legs,
Trying to navigate the way.

Little girl, you need to learn,
Little girl, what it is to be a woman

Laura is singing my thoughts at 2am

I need to know what it means to be a woman.

What is it to be a Woman?
An answer beyond binary and biology
An answer beyond archetypes and stereotypes.

Because all the stories of womanhood I have been told
Talk about belonging and giving. Belonging to someone/
Giving-up/giving-in.

Success is never just success. It is a signpost located on Rikers Island;
You can just about spot it through the fog.

Career girl is synonymous with isolated, alone, single.
Synonymous with aggressive, 'ballsy', pushy.
Synonymous with Unfulfilled.

Housewife is synonymous with wasted academia.
"Why did we bother to send her to school?"
Synonymous with intrigue and envy,
Is she doing what society told her to
Or what she wanted to do?

Then there's The Juggler:
Synonymous with YOU CAN HAVE IT ALL!
Synonymous with exhausted.
Synonymous with mother missing from memories.

Woman, O, Woman.
Woe it is to be woman,
Wow it is to be woman!

You can't seem to say woman without Mother:
Sister
Daughter
Wife
Mistress
Lover

In these occupations we're supposed to find our fulfilment
Merit and honour.

But the Compass in me is guiding me to something Bigger,
Something deeper.

It says Womanhood is synonymous with Contradiction.
Synonymous with Yours.
Stamp the blueprint of your essence all over your experience.

The womanhood you have been gifted with is unique,
But filled with commonalities.

Revel in your weaknesses
Bask in your strengths.

Chart your own course,
Follow the winds of your intuition and imagination.
Try to trust always,
But know when to have your guard up.

Love so fierce and sweeping
That forest fires will seem insignificant!
Know when to burn out
instead of being put out.

Know that womanhood is a sisterhood, you will be let down
and lifted-up.

Little girl you need to learn

Laura is still singing,
A thing of my doing.

Little girl, you need to learn,
Little girl, you need to learn what it is to be a woman.

Little girl you need to learn.
Womanhood is something you've already earned.

ACKNOWLEDGEMENTS

Firstly to Bernie, my AS English Lang and Lit teacher, without your encouragement to enter that poetry competition many moons ago, this book and all the poetry I have written since being 17 would most likely not exist. Getting published at that age gave me such a huge confidence boost to be able to put myself out there and claim my voice. It showed me that it wasn't just a love but also a talent. Thank you for believing in me and exposing me to so many fabulous poetic styles.

I want to express my profound gratitude to my family: my mother Sharon; you are one of my biggest inspirations in life. Thank you for feeding me books non-stop and telling me I could be anyone or anything I wanted to be as long as I worked at it. You were right mom!

My Dear brother Kevan, thank you for being my rock and quiet strength and all the magic and sci-fi you exposed be to growing up.

My dear sisters, Mel you were like a mother to me for so many years. Thank you for nourishing my mind and spirit growing up. San, my Kiki I'm so happy to have you by my side this lifetime, to grow and ascend with.

Sankofa is a pandemic baby. It was a time in my life when I really had time to sit and write (still heavily juggling but still more time). I mined my mind and heart, revisited over a decade's worth of work and wrote a lot of fresh pieces. Hundreds did not make the cut. Much like my EX and I, however I would still like to thank him for the copious cups of tea, food and reminders to sleep and bathe.

I am beyond grateful for the gift that poetry has been throughout my life, the many opportunities and adventures it has provided and continues to. I am most thankful though for the vehicle and voice it has given me and the catharsis it helps me provide to others.

Thank you to Beth and Adam without whom, physically, I would not have been able to write this book. During lockdown my laptop broke, I lost years' worth of work and couldn't afford to replace my laptop. Beth surprised me with an old Mac laptop after the movies! I may not have cried then but my heart was flooding with gratitude and love. They had heard of my plight and got one of Adam's brother's old laptops for me. I was able to produce many more magical pieces of poetry and work remotely because of this generous gift. It served me many years until it finally broke and I was able to replace it.

Thanks to my friends and fellow poets, who I could vent to about this process and who really got it: Nafeesa, Oakley, Shaun. Thank you for being trailblazers in my life, lighting the way and the path. I love y'all more than you know. Jess, with your huge supportive heart, thank you for being you and being there.

The same sentiments go to my soul sister Carmen. I couldn't imagine living this life without you, Bestie. Thank you for your wisdom in all situations.

Dear Scarlett, thanks for taking me under your wing at Fawn Press and letting me see what the other side of this publishing business is about. And for the homegrown workshops. You don't know how much they helped me get my mojo back and think about the world in a different way.

Darling Chadwick, since 2013 you have been one of the most fiercely supportive champions of my work and just me in general! Thank you so much, brother from another mother. You lifted me high when I didn't have the wings to fly. We will make our homeland proud with the art we produce.

To Kim and Amy, y'all really made 'Future Poets' out of us all! Thank you for the inspiration, the structure and just the badass, unapologetic, no-nonsense, 'get shit done' attitude you live with and inspired me with.

To Stuart, thank you for seeing the need in the poetry scene for something like Verve Poetry Press and Festival. You've really helped to put Birmingham and The Midlands on the map! On a personal level, a huge thank you for this opportunity and for flowing with me through all the ups and downs of doubt. I appreciate your belief in me and my work an infinite amount. Thanks for putting me on the map.

A huge thank you to Nina. You were the last missing piece in the birth of *Sankofa*. Thank you for the front cover. It is gorgeous. I had the vision in my mind but your execution and the way you diligently worked left me in awe! That image captures the Afro-Future, intersectional space dimension dreamland I was after but couldn't draw. Here's to the amazing children's books we will make together.

I would also like to thank the organisations over the years who have played a pivitol part in helping me develop as a poet and performer: MAC, Ideas Tap, Apples and Snakes. Thank you, Beatfreeks, for the many collectives like "Bellows or Beetroots" and the mentors such as Bohdan and Spoz. For the opportunities to grow, hone my craft and pass it back to the community. I'm still living with the ethos of "Collaborate, don't compete."

And last but certainly not least, I want to thank You, dear reader, for seeing my book, picking it up, reading it. I hope you found what you needed between the lines.

With all my love and gratitude.

ALSO AVAILABLE FROM VERVEPOETRYPRESS.COM

Into The Ordinary
Jemima Hughes

The brilliant second collection from Jemima - survival poetry to savour!

This is not out of the ordinary. This is commonplace.

Following on from her storming, debut poetry collection Unorthodox, Jemima Hughes sits with you in the aftermath to discuss how to rebuild. Jemima's story is one of sexual violence trauma and mental health difficulties but, ultimately, it is a story of hope.

Unorthodox was what happened. *Into the Ordinary* explores how we can make the world a more understanding, accepting and comfortable place for those living with these experiences.

'Jemima has a way of transporting you through darkness and into light in through her words and her performance. When she writes, she captures a reality that so many will find themselves in, and when she performs, she takes us all there.' - Casey Bailey

Available in paperback:
ISBN: 978 1 912565 40 1
100 pages • 216 x 138 • 30 poems
£10.99

ABOUT VERVE POETRY PRESS

Verve Poetry Press is an award-winning press that focused initially on meeting a local need in Birmingham - a need for the vibrant poetry scene here in Brum to find a way to present itself to the poetry world via publication. Co-founded by Stuart Bartholomew and Amerah Saleh, it now publishes poets from all corners of the UK - poets that speak to the city's varied and energetic qualities and will contribute to its many poetic stories.

Added to this is a colourful pamphlet series, many featuring poets who have performed at our sister festival - and a poetry show series which captures the magic of longer poetry performance pieces by festival alumni such as Polarbear, Matt Abbott and Imogen Stirling.

The press has been voted Most Innovative Publisher at the Saboteur Awards, and has won the Publisher's Award for Poetry Pamphlets at the Michael Marks Awards.

Like the festival, we strive to think about poetry in inclusive ways and embrace the multiplicity of approaches towards this glorious art.

www.vervepoetrypress.com
@VervePoetryPres
mail@vervepoetrypress.com